Stillness and Sparks

The Open-Anywhere Insight Book to Guide Your Day

A Happiness Recharge Book

A Happiness Recharge Book

Stillness and Sparks
The Open-Anywhere Insight Book to Guide Your Day

Copyright © 2025 by Kelly Stone Cramer

All rights reserved. This book or any portion thereof may not be reproduced or used in any manner whatsoever without the written permission of the author except for the use of brief quotations in a book review.

ISBN: 9798277944196

Content by Kelly Stone Cramer, founder of Happiness Recharge.

www.HappinessRecharge.com.

Legal Disclaimer
The content of this book is not intended to be for medical use. The author disclaims any liability for actions taken by the readers.

It is advisable to avoid doing anything you do not feel safe doing or something you are incapable of or is dangerous for your body. You know your body best and know what it is comfortable and what should be avoided. Trust and listen to yourself.

Please visit a healthcare professional if you need help (asking for support is a sign of great strength).

Take care of yourself always. Your well-being matters.

Preface

Welcome readers. The following is a gentle beginning and instructions on how to use this book. There are days when the world asks for more of you than you meant to give. And there are days when you can feel a small ember inside you, brightening, waiting for a breath of attention.

This book is a place for both.

Stillness lives in the pauses, the moments when you re-member yourself, when your shoulders drop without effort, when the noise of the world fades enough for your own voice to come forward.

Spark is the glimmer that follows a thought that warms you, a shift in direction, a truth you recognize as already yours.

You don't need to read this from beginning to end. Let your hands find any page. Let the message meet you exactly where you are. Some days you might seek clarity. Other days, comfort. Other days still, a gentle push toward what you're becoming.

Wherever you land, consider it your invitation for the day. A whisper. A nudge. A moment to breathe. This is a space of quiet embers. May you discover something here that lights your way.

Throughout these pages, you'll notice a small symbol beside each entry, which is a quiet guide of its own.

One symbol marks a moment of **Stillness**, offering you grounding, calm, and space to breathe.

Another marks a **Spark**, bringing a touch of energy, clarity, or gentle momentum for the day ahead.

Let these symbols help you feel your way through the book, choosing what you need most in each moment. Think of them as little lanterns along your path, illuminating whether it's time to soften or to shine a bit brighter.

The Open-Anywhere Insights

Anchor

What strengthens you? To know this is to hold a map back to yourself. As vital as naming what drains you is the wisdom of recognizing what fuels your fire—what stirs your spirit and steadies your soul. When you know what empowers you, you hold the key to your own becoming. Prioritizing it is the spark that sets your journey in motion; making it a habit is the rhythm that keeps your feet on solid ground. The question is not just if you'll walk this path, but if you'll be bold enough to carve it when none yet exists—because when you do, your own strength becomes the wind at your back.

Awaken

What if, to the extent your life allows, you began each day by honoring your own needs first? Imagine the quiet power of movement awakening your limbs, the nourishment of a meal chosen with care, the calm of a breath taken with purpose. Perhaps you'd write your thoughts into clarity, or lose time in a hobby that lights your spirit. The world won't pause—it will stay loud and hurried—but by devoting your first moments to yourself, you plant a flag of worthiness in the soil of your day. You say, "I matter," before the demands can say otherwise. And in doing so, your self-care becomes less of an afterthought and more of a foundation—quiet, steady, and alive.

Balance

When the mind finds its center, the world, too, seems to fall gently into place. Like ripples on a once-troubled pond, the chaos calms, and clarity returns. In imbalance, even the smallest gust can feel like a storm—tempests of anger, waves of stress. But when balance is restored, those same storms pass through like wind through trees—noticed, but no longer feared. This equilibrium isn't stumbled upon; it is cultivated through the quiet pursuit of joy, the soft rituals that stir the soul, the tender moments that bring peace and presence. Imagine a world where each heart was tuned to its own harmony, where balance was not an afterthought but a daily devotion. What grace might fill the air then—what beauty might bloom in the stillness of a mind at peace.

Be

You can't fast-forward life to rush to the so-called good parts, nor can you press pause to stretch the sweetness of what you love. Time is a fickle, untamable thing—slipping through fingers no matter how tightly you hold on. But in its passing, it reveals what matters most, where your love lives, what stirs your heart, and what you grieve when it's gone. You cannot sway time or bend it to your will, but you can meet each moment with presence. You can let it wash over you, imperfect and alive, and know that this, the here and now, is the only place you can be. So breathe and be.

Becoming

When feelings are drawn inward and given the shape of thought, life begins to transform—quietly, profoundly. You become an alchemist of emotion, a master of your inner tides, knowing yourself with a rare, radiant clarity. Few dare this path, fewer still realize it exists. Yet it holds the key to a superpower: the deep, honest knowing of the self. Through the lens of tenderness and courage, you begin to see where growth is calling, where truth is buried. And in that brave, gentle unfolding, you may discover the rarest treasure of all—the real you, the gift only you can unwrap.

Begin

Somewhere, midway through the long and winding journey, you may pause and realize — with a breathless wonder — that you are, in truth, only just at the beginning. Yet every step that carried you here, every stumble and soaring moment, was not for nothing. They were the unseen bridges stretched across vast terrain, each one built by your persistence, your dreams, your pain. Without them, you could not have crossed into this new dawn. The journey, it seems, was not just toward a destination, but toward the strength and knowing that now lets you truly begin.

Calling

Your calling may not come in a thunderous entrance, nor announce itself with trumpets or flashing signs. It may whisper through the rustle of curiosity, flicker in the quiet sparks of interest that tug at your heart when no one is watching. It may arrive disguised as a gentle nudge, a passing thought, a fleeting joy that returns again and again. The point is not to wait for certainty, but to notice—to pay attention to those subtle breadcrumbs scattered across your days. Follow them with wonder, with courage, down winding paths and hidden trails. For often it is in the smallest inklings that the soul begins to remember its way home.

Calm

Notice, now, the moments you reach for chaos over calm—the scramble to do too much, to be too much, to give too much, to stretch yourself thin across the impossible. Do you race to meet every need while neglecting your own, wearing busyness like a badge? What if, instead, you let calm be your compass? What if peace became the measure by which you shaped your choices? In each breath lies a doorway back. So ask yourself often and gently, when you feel tense or stressed: How can I add calm to this moment? Perhaps this mantra can ease your days: With each breath, I choose calm. I bring peace to this moment—because I can, and I embody calm.

Challenges

The bad days, though heavy and uninvited, carry a quiet power—they are kindling for the soul, fuel to reignite the fire of forgotten hopes, to redraw the lines of our boundaries, and to rekindle a deeper appreciation for the light we often take for granted. They teach us contrast, so we may truly savor the warmth of joy, the calm of peace, and the rare brilliance of the best days. Yet in their shadowed presence, we must tread gently. For while it is healing to feel sorrow, to let anger or grief pass through like a storm, it is dangerous to let them build a home where serenity is meant to dwell. The night may fall, but we are not meant to stay there; we are meant to rise with the dawn, wiser, steadier, and more attuned to the light.

Choose

Life, in its winding wisdom, tugs at the edges of our soul, pulling us down roads both radiant and rough. Some trails are lined with blossoms of hope, while others cut like thorns—painful, persistent, yet profoundly telling. These are not just struggles, but sacred signals, gentle alarms echoing from within, urging us to pause, to pivot, to protect our peace. In the chaos and clamor, there lies a quiet truth: the most powerful decision we can ever make is to honor ourselves. Choose what heals you. Choose what helps you grow. Choose the kind of love that begins with you. Choose to rest when the world demands more. Choose light when shadows loom large. No matter where your feet wander, let your heart return to this—make room, always, to choose you.

Compassion

It's important to love one another with compassion, for beneath every smile lies a story, and behind every silence, a struggle. We are all a mosaic of cracks and mended pieces, stitched together by time, pain, and fleeting moments of grace. If only we could glimpse the invisible scars carved by life's weight — the heartbreaks, the losses, the quiet battles — we might cradle each other's souls with gentler hands. We are, each of us, yearning to be seen, to be known, to be told we matter in this chaotic dance of existence. But what if, instead of waiting to be validated, we became the ones who offered warmth first? A word, a glance, a kindness — tiny sparks that could light the dark corners of someone's day. Imagine a world where love wasn't rationed, but poured freely, where judgment gave way to understanding. What a softer, braver world that would be.

Courage

Perhaps when fears refuse to be vanquished, they ask instead to be met—with courage steady and perseverance true. Though we long to hush the tremble of discomfort, to ease the ache of anxious hearts, there is quiet glory in simply showing up, again and again, with hope that each step widens the walls of what once felt small. For courage is not the absence of fear, but the rhythm of a heart that keeps beating, strong not by chance, but by constant, brave use.

Creating

Creation is not a race toward some distant finish line, but a quiet unfolding, a slow dance with time itself. It is the art of stillness in motion, of moving so gently through each moment that the world begins to whisper its secrets. In the hush of unhurried effort, every texture, every breath, every flicker of light reveals its meaning. This is not the path of haste, but of depth — where each step is deliberate, each pause sacred. And in surrendering to this pace, the process becomes its own guide, carrying you not with force, but with grace, to a finish line that feels less like an end and more like a becoming.

Defiance

To live fully is to prove fate wrong for another day—to rise with defiance in your breath and wonder in your bones, to take the script the world handed you and scribble joy into its margins. It is to greet the morning as if it were not promised and still offer it your whole heart, to dance on the edge of the unknown with laughter that echoes louder than fear. Each choice to love, to create, to be present is a quiet rebellion against the shadows that say you cannot, should not, will not. And yet, here you are—living as if you belong to the stars and not to the limits fate once tried to write in stone.

Destiny

You were given this life for a reason—a purpose woven into the very thread of your being, though its shape may forever elude your grasp. It is not your fate to chase after meaning like a shadow just beyond the light, nor to unravel every secret held in the folds of time. No, your true destiny is far simpler, far braver: to live. To breathe in each sunrise as if it were your first, to meet each moment not with certainty, but with courage. For in the act of living—fully, fiercely, presently—you fulfill the reason, even if you never name it.

Dream

How could you ever know the taste of joy if you had not first dared to dream? Dreams are the tender seeds planted in the soil of the soul, watered by hope and warmed by longing. They reach upward, stretching fragile stems toward the sun of possibility. Without them, the heart would forget how to lift itself beyond the weight of the world. It is in dreaming that we prepare ourselves for wonder, and it is only through wonder that true joy can bloom.

Ease

To constantly push against your limits, to always strive and stretch, may seem like the path to growth – but without pause, the beauty of the present slips quietly through your fingers. There is a sacred art in softening, in loosening the grip and letting grace take your hand. When you release the pressure to always achieve, the breath returns, deep and grounding. Your nervous system, no longer on high alert, begins to hum a quieter song–one of safety, of rest, of truth. And in that stillness, something remarkable happens: life begins to unfold not from force, but from flow. You begin to live not as a performance, but as a presence. Not a striving self, but a truer one-unmasked, unhurried, and finally at peace.

Embodiment

Trust your body—it is wise beyond measure, a quiet miracle in motion. Trust its whispers, the language of fatigue, hunger, ache, and renewal. Trust the way it heals, not on demand, but on time, and how movement can stir the still waters of your soul. You do not need to earn your body's worth by matching it to another's shape. Worthiness lives in your breath, your heartbeat, your being. Let rest be sacred, not shameful. Speak for your body when the world forgets its limits. Listen, honor, respond—and you will find your way back to feeling whole. This vessel, this home, is not just flesh; it is spirit wrapped in skin, deserving of your deepest care.

Explore

Exploration belongs to everyone—not just those chasing distant horizons or buried gold, but to every soul brave enough to journey inward. The truest explorers listen first to the quiet longings of the heart, then dare to step into the unknown with hope as their compass. And even if the path they choose leads to a door they no longer wish to open, the voyage is never wasted—for to know what is not your way is still a sacred kind of knowing, and every turn, even away, is a step toward truth.

Expand

While you may feel like a tiny fleck in this vast galactic riddle, remember—you were forged from the same fire as stars. You are not separate from the cosmos but a living breath of it, walking around in a body made of ancient light. So what force on Earth could truly stand against you? You, who were born a miracle on this spinning stone, carried forth from the infinite to face the finite. You come from power, from wonder, from the very fabric of what makes the universe expand. So let no doubt linger—if you can emerge from that celestial chaos into form, you can rise through anything.

Fear

The root of fear, curiously, can be love—tender and unyielding. For in the trembling of uncertainty lies the depth of care, and in the ache of what could be lost blooms the quiet beauty of what is held dear. Fear does not always signal weakness; sometimes it is the soul's whisper that something precious dwells nearby. Without this sacred tension, one might drift untouched by the profound solace that only love can grant—a warmth that seeps deep into the heart and lingers in the corners of the soul, quietly completing us.

Fire

Anger is the ancient key that unlocks the gate to your fire warrior—fierce, radiant, and unrelenting. When summoned, they rise in a blaze, eyes like molten stars, breath like burning wind, capable of scorching the very earth with a single cry. Their fury dazzles, terrifies, and protects. But peer beyond the brilliance, and you'll find a core less rage than raw ache—a wound buried deep, wrapped tightly in armor forged from ego, pride, and sorrow. These layers are not weakness but shield, grown over time to keep the old pain from bleeding anew. And so, when the fire warrior appears, the question is not how to silence them—but how to listen. Do you bow to their flames and let them reign unchecked, or dare to peel back the searing shell and ask, gently, where it hurts?

Flow

To honor your flow is as like drinking water from a pure, living spring. Each action taken in alignment with your true self nourishes something deep within, something ancient and quietly burning. With every choice that mirrors your soul's rhythm, your purpose is quenched, refreshed like parched earth after long-awaited rain. To follow your flow is to listen to life itself, to sip from the endless current of meaning that runs beneath all things, and in doing so, to thrive.

Forward

Sometimes the bravest thing you can do is simply stand where you are—and take one honest step forward. It takes a quiet, steady courage to face life exactly as it unfolds, without flinching, without fleeing, without pretending it's something else. To meet your moments head-on is not a promise of victory, but it is a vow to your truest self. And that vow matters. Listen closely to the pulse of your own heart, that inner compass of truth. Let it guide you with fierce grace and necessary rest. Even slow strides, taken in truth, will carry you further in the world.

Fun

What a joyous dance life becomes when you discover the things that set your soul ablaze. When you uncover what lights you up from within, every moment starts to shimmer with possibility. And oh, the fun—pure, boundless fun—when you place those passions at the top of your list, giving them your time, your energy, your presence. In those sacred moments of delight, you catch a glimpse of who you truly are: playful as the wind, lighthearted as sunlight on water, and endlessly kind. The more you follow that spark, the more you return to the radiant essence you were always meant to be.

Heal

It takes a brave heart to heal—for healing is no gentle path, but a storm-weathered journey through shadows of pain, through echoes of suffering that linger in the bones. To mend, one must move beyond the pride that guards old wounds and the ego that fears their exposure. It begins with surrender—an aching stillness, the uneasy acceptance of what is. And from that stillness rises resilience, fierce and flickering like dawn light after a sleepless night. You press on, not in leaps, but in quiet, stubborn inches—step by step toward a horizon unseen, yet deeply felt. With each breath, you reshape your world, daring to believe in softer days, in lighter burdens, in a life made whole not despite the scars, but because of them.

Ignition

And suddenly, you existed—as if the universe exhaled and in that breath, you were born. Like a flame catching spark in the hush of dark, you flickered into being, radiant with possibility. What does the world look like now that you're here? Does it soften in your kindness, shift gently beneath your care? Do your words lift others, even when unspoken, your presence creating quiet echoes of hope? Whether your ripples stretch wide or stay tenderly near, may they carry light wherever they fall. You are not here by accident. You are a constellation in motion—shining, shaping, becoming—if only you dare to glow.

Kindness

Kindness is not a grand display, but a quiet revolution. It's the soft word when tempers rise, the steady hand when someone stumbles, the unseen gesture that says, "You matter." It doesn't demand recognition, yet it changes everything it touches. Kindness is the thread that mends what's torn, the light that glows in another's darkness. It lives in the pauses—in listening without rushing, in forgiving without needing to be asked, in seeing the soul beneath the surface. To be kind is to recognize the sacred in others, even when they forget it in themselves. It is not weakness, but courage—a deliberate choice to lead with heart in a world that often forgets how.

Legacy

Perhaps life was never meant to be a grand stage upon which we build towering legacies to outlast our names. No, the true legacy breathes in the moments we make today matter — in the tender, unrepeatable now. It is crafted not through conquest, but through the quiet courage to loosen the grip of ego, to befriend the trembling spirit of bravery, and to say yes — again and again — to the endless unfolding of growth. In every direction life pulls us, whether into sorrow or into wonder, we are invited to lean in, to trust, and to weave a legacy made of living fully, not merely lasting long.

Listen

Waiting for answers from the Divine? But don't you see—life itself is the Divine, speaking in whispers and sacred echoes through every heartbeat, every shared glance, every word exchanged between souls. Your conversations, whether with strangers, loved ones, or the still voice within, are not merely moments—they are the Divine responding, shaping, revealing. Even your thoughts, those silent ripples within, rise like tides pulled by celestial forces, bearing messages meant only for you. So pause. Breathe. Be still. The Divine is not distant—it speaks through you, within you, all around you. Are you truly listening?

Meaning

Self-acceptance, in all its quiet strength, opens the door to discernment. When you truly honor your limitations and preferences—not as flaws, but as the sacred boundaries of your truth—you begin to curate your life with care. You choose the who that nourishes you, the what that aligns, the how that supports your rhythm, the when that respects your pace, and the where that feels like home. But most of all, you uncover the why—the deep pulse beneath it all. With that clarity, life takes on a steadier beat, and each step becomes an act of intention. You are no longer just moving— you are moving with meaning.

Momentum

Each day holds the makings of a masterpiece—if only you dare to notice. Not for perfection, nor for goals all met, but for the quiet triumphs: the effort given, the lessons learned, the simple act of showing up. Let progress be enough for joy to bloom. If celebration waits only at the finish line, you'll miss the brilliance of the path itself. So breathe in the now, honor the soul doing its best, and follow the sparks of joy—they are the brushstrokes that color your life.

Peaceful

Peace isn't only found in the quiet corners where you explore pauses—it lives, too, in the heart of your everyday rhythm. It doesn't wait for you at the edge of a retreat or hide behind a distant weekend. It pulses beneath the noise. Yes, it takes focus and intention—to sift through calendar chaos, to soften the sharp edges of urgency, to remember that not every fire is yours to put out. But with gentle practice, peace can become a thread in the fabric of your daily life—a quiet steadying your breath, guiding your choices, and reminding you that serenity isn't an escape; it's a way of being, even as the world spins on. All the while, your world can spin peacefully.

Perspective

Sometimes the wisest move is not to press forward, but to pause—to step back and let the weight fall away for a moment. Like holding a puzzle too close, struggle can blur the pieces; but with distance, patterns emerge. It's not the break itself that mends, but the breath it offers—the room it creates for clarity to return. In that space between tension and release, the mind softens, the heart steadies, and your values rise again like stars through a clearing sky. With fresh eyes, what once seemed tangled begins to loosen, and you remember not just what you're facing, but who you are as you face it.

Pivot

Sometimes, stepping away from the familiar rhythm of our daily routines can spark a quiet, yet profound, renewal within. Like a flame that momentarily fades, the stillness offers a chance for the embers to glow brighter, reigniting the very passions that once fueled our drive. In the space between the ordinary, we find the quiet magic that stirs our hearts, reminding us of what we love, what we long for, and what we are capable of creating once more. It is in this pause, this gentle pivot, that we rediscover the spark to fuel the fire anew.

Practice

Establishing a habit of practicing your art—or whatever outlet stirs your spirit—is like gently turning the tap each day, allowing a steady stream to run so the pipes never rust. Though not every drop will sparkle with brilliance, the act itself wards off stagnation, keeping the channel open and ready. In the quiet rhythm of showing up, you welcome the extraordinary, clearing a path for inspiration to find you—not as a sudden storm, but as a guest who knows they're always welcome.

Presence

To be organized is to lay a gentle hand upon the storm—to sort the scattered leaves of life into quiet piles, each one a small offering to peace. It is the art of clearing the altar of the mind, so presence may kneel there without distraction. In the hush that follows order, time stretches its limbs and breathes more deeply. Suddenly, the world slows—each moment gleams with clarity, like dew on morning grass. Through this simple tending, the soul is freed to listen, to linger, to truly be—not in haste, but in reverence.

Progress

You are enough—always have been, always will be. Don't let the quiet whispers of doubt, those shadows in your mind, dim the light of your becoming. As you walk this winding road of growth, remember: your dreams are vast because your spirit is vast, and though the journey ahead may stretch far beyond the horizon, every step—no matter how small—is a testament to your strength. You are moving, becoming, unfolding. Whether you leap forward or inch ahead, each movement is sacred. Progress is not always loud or fast, but it is always real. Trust in the rhythm of your travel as you make progress down along your path.

Purpose

Purpose doesn't always bloom where the world plants its seeds — not in the tidy rows of family tradition, nor in the neat furrows carved by society's steady hand, nor even in the shallow expectations you once held for yourself. No. Sometimes, purpose rises wild and untamed, spilling color beyond the lines, calling from the unexpected corners of curiosity — in a forgotten hobby, a whispered passion, a spark you never thought to chase. It is in those quiet rebellions that dreamers are born — those who stray from the paved roads and dare to carve new paths through untouched landscapes of possibility.

Reason

From the day you were born, you were dealt a losing hand. You'll lose youth to time, loved ones to their demise, and ultimately you'll lose your own current existence too. So why live at all? Why admire fiery sunsets that spill colors onto the sky? Why love so deeply you feel like you're lifted with floating wonder? Why learn new things to be able to apply it to your growth and wisdom? Why enjoy yourself doing the things that fill you to fuel your passions and aspirations? Why indeed? While everything has an end, perhaps your here and now is reason enough for it all.

Rebellion

In an unjust world, what is there to do but live—live boldly, wildly, and true. Breathe deeply into the marrow of your being, and let your days be more than survival. Let your presence take up space, not in defiance but in declaration: I am here, and I matter. Love who you love with a heart unguarded, unshaken by judgment. Seek what sets your spirit alight and chase it like the sun, with both hands open and trembling. Let your joy be fierce, your laughter uncontained. Let your quiet moments speak volumes, and your loud ones echo with meaning. Be a refuge for others, offer your strength when theirs runs low, and hold space for tenderness to grow in barren places. Be a witness to beauty and a participant in hope. Build, mend, nurture, rebel—in the smallest of ways or with grand, sweeping strokes. Let your choices reflect not only the world you were given, but the world you dare to believe in. And through it all, live—not in spite of the injustice, but as a living, breathing answer to it. Let your life say, This is what could be. Let your being become a protest of light.

Recenter

Sometimes life whirls with such velocity that it leaves you dizzy—spinning through days that blur together, swept along by demands that seem to choose you rather than the other way around. In the rush, it's easy to slip into reactivity, to feel more like a passenger than the captain of your own story. But even in the thick of it, the still truth remains: you hold the power of choice. It may take intention, even resistance, to carve out time for what nourishes your soul, to say no when your spirit whispers enough, or to pause for one long, conscious breath. Yet these are your quiet revolutions—moments when you reclaim your place at the helm, steering not by urgency, but by what matters most.

Resilience

Fatigue can be a symptom of a busy life—an echo of all the weight you carry, the roles you juggle, the hearts you tend to, and the deadlines you chase. So the next time your breath shortens and your shoulders tighten beneath the pressure, pause. Rather than scold yourself for reaching your limit, offer a quiet bow to the strength it took to arrive there. Let pride bloom in the places self-criticism used to dwell. You are not breaking—you are stretched by purpose, moved by effort, and alive in the doing.

Resonance

Joy and relaxation are not just feelings—they are medicine for your body, quieting the hum of your nervous system like a gentle lullaby. When your mind softens, your body follows, and that calm begins to ripple outward, touching everything around you with unseen grace. It is not your duty to soothe the world, but by tending to your own peace, you become a quiet invitation for others to do the same. In choosing joy, in honoring ease, you offer the world a softer place to land— and that, without even trying, is how you begin to change it.

Ride

You cannot summon a wave at will, nor bend the tide to meet your need—but you can learn its rhythm. With practice, with courage, with a heart open to the deep, you become not the master of the sea, but the one who moves with it. Life, like water, flows on its own terms. It will not yield to force, but it will meet you in motion if you dare to ride it—balanced not by control, but by surrender shaped into skill.

Rhythm

A balanced life is not born of constant ease or perpetual struggle, but of the sacred sway between the two. It is an ever-shifting tide, where stillness and challenges take turns shaping your life. To live only in comfort breeds stagnation, just as living only in hardship erodes the nervous system. But when you learn to tune into your own rhythm—honoring when to rest and when to rise—you begin to move with the music of your life, whether it plays a familiar song or a new, uncertain tune. Each step, stumble, and spin becomes part of a greater choreography, one that doesn't demand perfection, only presence. For while balance is a lifelong art, it is the willingness to keep dancing that brings the heart to find joy.

Sanctuary

Finding calm in a world that whirls and crashes like the sea is a quiet kind of triumph—a grace earned, not given. It's the art of noticing beauty in the swell of chaos, of carving space for stillness even as the tide pulls you forward. Peace comes not all at once, but in rhythms, like breath or moonlight—appearing, receding, returning again. As you shift and stretch with life's ever-changing tides, so too can your heart learn to anchor. In that anchoring, there is room for a calm mind, a softened body, an open heart—each a small sanctuary in motion.

Savor

To rush toward the finish is to blur the colors of the present—to bypass the nectar of love, the spark of joy, the quiet gifts tucked in daily moments. In our hurry to round life's next corner, we forsake the golden glimmers of connection, the tender echoes of self we only hear when still. Even pain has wisdom folded within it, lessons that fortify the soul for what's ahead. When we skip past now, we risk arriving unready. But when we soften our stride, letting life wash over us—its sharpness, its wonder, its wild bloom—we gather what is meant to be gathered, leaving nothing unlived or unseen.

Shift

When stress and struggle are flung like stones in your path—when aches, troubles, and tangled knots of life arrive uninvited—it's easy to slump beneath their weight, to dwell in the ache and call it home. But while sorrow has its season, staying there dims your strength. So when the next wave rises, try turning toward it not with dread, but with a curious eye—what can be done, where is the light? Let frustration be a compass, not a cage. Knowing your boundaries, holding close what you truly desire, can shift the storm from something you endure to something you navigate—with clarity as your helm.

Soothe

When calm feels distant and the world grows too heavy to hold, let that be your cue to self-soothe. In the hush of a warm blanket, the steam of tea curling like a breath of comfort, the gentle press of a pet against your side—these are the quiet rituals that steady the soul. A song that knows your heart, a show that wraps you in story, a journal that listens without judgment—all become lifelines in the swell of storm. Whether through movement, nourishment, or simple stillness, may you find the anchors that keep you from drifting too far. Let your soothing not be an afterthought, but a devotion—a soft and steady vow to tend to yourself when the waters rise.

Sowing

You cannot force lessons to bloom before their time, nor rush wisdom from seeds still taking root. Understanding ripens in its own season, not by will but by quiet unfolding. You cannot wring truth from what's only half-formed, but you can tend the soil of your own becoming—patiently, curiously. Observe the ache of wanting answers, the stir of restlessness for what's next, and let it soften you. In the space between knowing and not knowing, there is life to be lived: try something new, return to the sacred familiar, let joy slip in through unnoticed cracks. For while you wait, you're not standing still—you're growing, and in time, the insights will come like birds returning in spring, not because you chased them, but because you stayed.

Strength

True human strength lies in the symbolic heart. To lead with the heart is to envision a goal not yet real, to fix one's gaze upon a distant light and believe warmth will be reached. It is to hope with such intensity that the soul is compelled to leap from solid heights, often without the assurance of a safety net below. These are not reckless leaps, but sacred ones, fueled by trust in possibility. The more it's used, the stronger the heart becomes—allowing one to become braver, more open, more alive.

Stillness

Making time for what steadies you becomes more than a habit—it becomes a sanctuary, a quiet harbor in the storm of life. It's in these moments, however small or subtle, that you return to yourself. Here, in the softness of peace or the still hush of deep thought, you find more than rest—you find renewal. Perhaps it's a rhythm you've kept unknowingly, a sacred ritual disguised as a simple act: a walk, a song, a journal page, a breath. It need not be grand or visible to the world. Its power lies in the way it anchors your spirit, offers you clarity, and reminds you who you are beneath the noise. This gentle act, this chosen steadiness, becomes your foundation—one that holds you firm, so you can move through life with presence, with poise, and with grace.

Stress

Stress often springs from the aching sense of lost control—a tide that surges beyond our reach. Yet to endure it, even to transcend it, one must learn not to fight the wave, but to ride it with quiet grace. Become the watchful observer of the sea within, witnessing its rhythm without drowning in its pull. Remember always: you are one human, finite and fallible, but also resilient. You can only do what you can do—and that is enough. Let the tide rise and recede. Let it whisper its storms and silences. And through it all, stand firm in the truth of who you are: not the tide, but the shore.

Today

Today, you step closer to yourself — the truest, brightest self you already are. Now is the time for gentleness, to embrace your body, your mind, your life as they are. Only through acceptance will the path unfold, guiding you toward the even greater you of tomorrow.

Truth

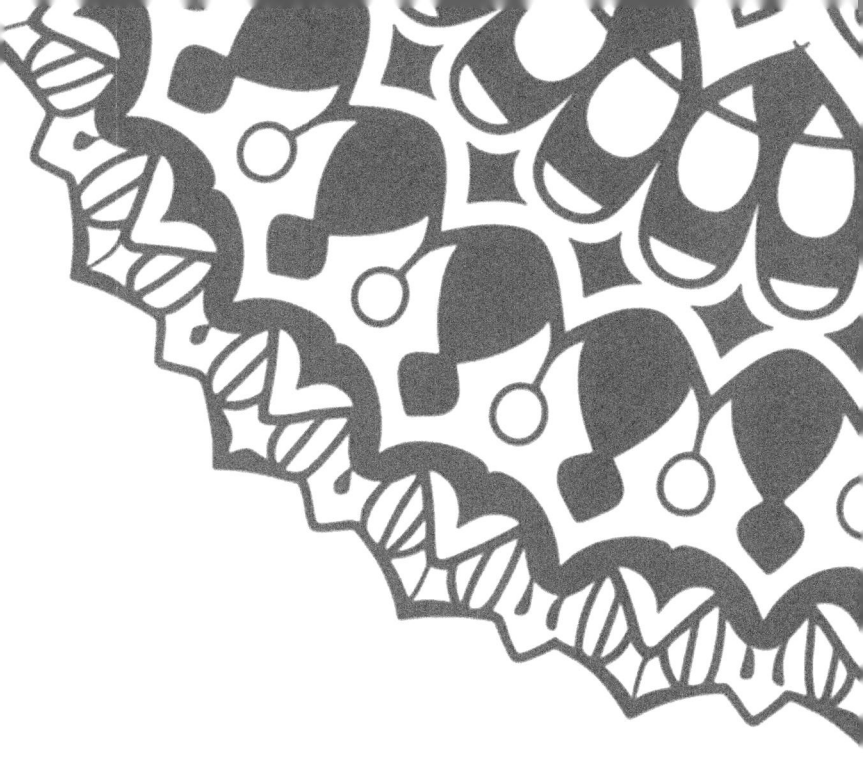

When you dare to express your truth — whether through emotions or shared words — you stir the stagnant air around you. The heaviness that once clouded your path begins to lift, revealing trails of light and possibility that were hidden in silence. Every feeling unveiled, every thought released, is a stone moved from the road ahead, clearing the way for your soul to journey forward, free and unburdened. In speaking your heart, you become both the seeker and the light that guides the way.

Unknown

Walking into the unknown is not merely a step into darkness, but a sacred journey into the vast and hidden chambers of your own becoming. It is the quiet courage to face uncertainty with open hands, to welcome the lessons whispered by mystery. In each shadow, a seed of wisdom is sown; in every stumble, a deeper strength is discovered. What you uncover there—about the world, about yourself—becomes a compass not just for the moment, but for all the days that follow, illuminating the path with purpose, clarity, and the ever-growing light of your potential.

Unwind

To constantly push against your limits, to always strive and stretch, may seem like the path to growth—but without pause, the beauty of the present slips quietly through your fingers. There is a sacred art in softening, in loosening the grip and letting grace take your hand. When you release the pressure to always achieve, the breath returns, deep and grounding. Your nervous system, no longer on high alert, begins to hum a quieter song—one of safety, of rest, of truth. And in that stillness, something remarkable happens: life begins to unfold not from force, but from flow. You begin to live not as a performance, but as a presence. Not a striving self, but a truer one—unmasked, unhurried, and finally at peace.

Uprising

Life can hurl you to the ground with such force you'd swear the earth trembled beneath your fall, and yet—miraculously—you bounce. Bruised, maybe. Shaken, surely. But not broken. In those moments, when shadows stretch long and heavy across your spirit, even the quietest thank you becomes a roar of resilience. To name one thing—just one glimmer, one breath, one bird still singing—is not weakness, but strength rising from the rubble. Yes, you may be knocked off your stoop, pride cracked, heart sore—but look at you: still here, still breathing, a quiet miracle in motion.

Whole

When you name your own limitations, you loosen their grip—they no longer lurk as silent burdens, but become stepping stones for growth. In the light of your acknowledgment, they shrink, no longer towering hurdles but invitations to evolve. What you own, no one can use against you; your honesty becomes your armor. To stand in full truth, in the glow of both your struggles and your strengths, is to rise in quiet power—rooted, whole, and unshakably you.

Wisdom

Spring flowers remind us that life returns, even after the coldest season—rising from frozen earth with quiet resilience, they bloom not in haste, but in time. Trees, bent by the weight of heavy winds, show us that strength lies in the willingness to bend, not break; that rootedness and surrender can coexist. And lakes, ever shifting, reflect the world honestly—serene beneath clear skies, wild beneath storms—teaching us that it's natural to respond, to feel, to move with what surrounds us. In their rhythms, nature whispers a gentle truth: that renewal, flexibility, and emotional depth are not weaknesses, but the sacred ways life endures. Nature has endless wisdom as everything has its season, even you.

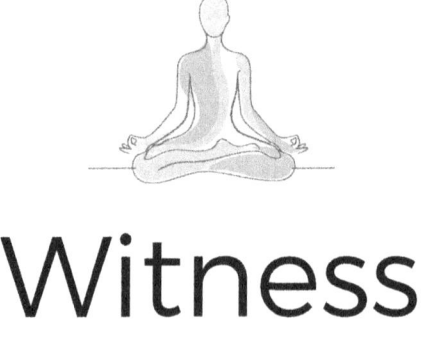

Witness

To be your own witness amid the darker tides of thought is to offer yourself a rare and sacred gift — the gift of seeing without judgment. In the quiet act of observation, the shadowed corners of your mind are gently illuminated, no longer left to fester in silence. It is within this tender light that wisdom takes root, growing slowly, deliberately, like a tree reaching for the sun. And from this wisdom, a deeper kindness blooms — a kindness first toward yourself, and then, like ripples across water, toward the whole aching world.

A Gentle Closing (until you return)

You've wandered through these pages in your own time, following the threads that called to you. Whether you arrived seeking calm, clarity, encouragement, or simply a soft moment to yourself, I hope something here met you with warmth.

Remember that the insights you found aren't meant to be carried perfectly—only held lightly.
Let them settle where they will. Let them shift with you. Let them spark new thoughts long after you close the book.

When your days feel hurried, or when you lose your footing, or when you simply want a quiet companion, you can return. Open anywhere. Begin again. The stillness and the spark will always be here, waiting to greet you.

Thank you for spending this time within these pages.
May the path ahead feel a little brighter, a little steadier, and lit with small, meaningful moments of your own making.

Go gently.
And come back whenever you wish.

Find more books at **www.HappinessRecharge.com**.

Made in the USA
Coppell, TX
10 January 2026

67549868R00080